THIS JOURNAL
BELONGS TO

...THERE IS NO
SUBSTITUTE FOR
GOING OUT TO THE
MOVIES. THERE IS

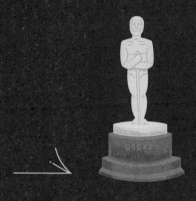

MOVIES ARE LIKE MAGIC TRICKS.

— *JEFF BRIDGES* —

YOU CAN MAP YOUR LIFE
THROUGH YOUR FAVORITE
MOVIES, AND NO TWO
PEOPLE'S MAPS WILL
BE THE SAME.

—— *MARY SCHMICH* ——

CINEMA SHOULD MAKE
YOU FORGET YOU ARE
SITTING IN A THEATER.

—— ROMAN POLANSKI ——

IT'S NOT WHAT A MOVIE IS ABOUT, IT'S HOW IT IS ABOUT IT.

—— *ROGER EBERT* ——

CINEMA IS A MATTER OF WHAT'S IN THE FRAME AND WHAT'S OUT.

— MARTIN SCORSESE —

IT'S THE STORY
THAT COUNTS.

— VINCENTE MINNELLI —

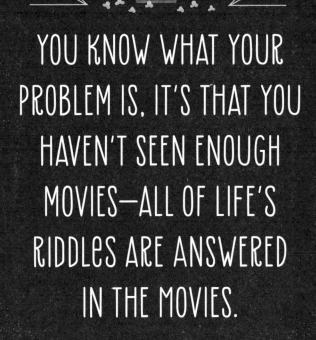

YOU KNOW WHAT YOUR
PROBLEM IS, IT'S THAT YOU
HAVEN'T SEEN ENOUGH
MOVIES—ALL OF LIFE'S
RIDDLES ARE ANSWERED
IN THE MOVIES.

— STEVE MARTIN —